CRAVE.FEAR.RISE

"The basic blueprint to rise, no matter who you are or what stands in your way, success is within reach."

Sahaya Jaison M

Made with ♥ on the Notion Press Platform

www.notionpress.com

CONTENTS

NOTE

This book is not a PhD thesis or a deep dive into life's mysteries. It's a simple, straightforward guide, stitched together from the lessons I've learned the hard way. I've kept it basic, no overly complicated theories or endless examples to bore you. Why? Because I'm not some subject matter expert handing out life hacks from a pedestal. I'm just someone who's been through the trenches and figured out a few things worth sharing.

When I bought my first book, it felt like deciphering a foreign language. Too many big words, too many examples, and honestly, it made me want to shut the book and take a nap. So, I decided to write something that people like me, people like us, would actually read.

This book is for people like us, the 18 to 21 crowd who are navigating life's mess of emotions, ambitions, and uncertainties. At 20, I know how it feels. The confusion of what's next, the excitement of figuring it out, the fear of failing, and the drive to keep going. I've packed this book with relatable chapters and real stories to show you that if I can make progress, so can you.

If you're looking for overly complex theories or magic formulas for success, this isn't right book. But if you want relatable advice, simple guidance, and a sense of connection, you've come to the right book.

Introduction

If you fail to upgrade,
you're like an old mobile that lags but still works.

Why I Wrote This Book

By writing this book, I'm not claiming to be the smartest person in the world and by reading it, you won't magically become one either. But that's not the point. This is a self-development book, and its goal is to help you become better, not perfect, not flawless, just better.

The Professor Who Stopped Learning

Dr. Robert was a professor at one of the most prestigious institutes. He held two PhDs, four bachelor's degrees, and three master's degrees, and had guided several scholars. In his mind, he was the most knowledgeable person in the entire institute.

On June 24, 2024, he was invited as a guest speaker by the history and economics department of another university. His topic? "Petro-Dollar and Global Trade." For 30 minutes, he delivered a compelling lecture, concluding confidently that no currency could ever replace the US dollar in international trade.

The audience applauded. He felt proud, as usual. Then, it was time for questions.

A young student, Isak Paul, raised his hand. The mic was passed to him.

Isak: "Good evening, sir. I'm Isak Paul. My question is: Can the BRICS nations replace the US dollar's dominance? I read recently that they're planning to introduce a gold-backed common currency."

Professor Robert: *"Good evening, Isak. Interesting question. In my opinion, BRICS cannot replace the US dollar. Even if five countries avoid the dollar, it won't affect its dominance."*

Isak: "Sir, I'd like to correct you. As of January 1, 2024, BRICS expanded to nine countries."

The professor hesitated. "I wasn't aware of that update," he admitted. "But still, nine countries won't shake the dollar's position."

Isak: "Sir, BRICS includes three major crude oil producers Russia, Iran, and the UAE. It also includes two of the largest consumers, India and China. India has already started buying oil in its local currency, and China is increasing its non-dollar trades. If BRICS launches a common currency, wouldn't it disrupt the petrodollar system?"

Dr. Robert paused. "You're right, Isak," he said. "I've been so confident in my knowledge that I stopped learning. I thought I knew everything, but today I realize that holding degrees means nothing if you don't stay curious. Thank you for reminding me."

Lessons from the Story:

1. **Confidence with Humility:** No matter who your opponent is, if you know you're right, stand your ground. But do it with respect.
2. **Never Stop Learning:** Your degrees don't define your knowledge. If you stop learning, you become outdated.
3. **Admit When You're Wrong:** Acknowledging someone else's correctness isn't a loss, it's growth.
4. **Argue to Learn, Not to Win:** Winning an argument might boost your ego, but learning from it builds character.

Let me share an another story

The Two Giants: Yahoo vs. Google

In the late 1990s, Yahoo was the king of the internet. It was the go-to platform for search, email, and news. If you had an internet connection, you knew Yahoo. Around the same time, two young men, Larry Page and Sergey Brin, came up with a new way to rank web pages based on their relevance. They called it Google.

Yahoo had the resources, the market share, and the influence. Google had a fresh idea and a hunger to innovate.

By the early 2000s, Yahoo had the opportunity to buy Google for $1 million. But Yahoo laughed it off. "We're already the leaders," they thought. "Why should we invest in some startup with a weird name?"

Fast forward a decade. While Google was constantly evolving bringing new technologies like Gmail, Google Maps, and YouTube into the fold Yahoo stuck to its old ways. They underestimated the speed of technological change and overestimated their market dominance.

By the time Yahoo realized they were falling behind, it was too late. Google has become a global giant, revolutionizing not just search engines but how the world communicates, learns, and does business. Meanwhile, Yahoo faded into irrelevance, becoming a cautionary tale for anyone too comfortable to adapt.

Moral:

Just like Yahoo, if you stop adapting and evolving, you risk becoming irrelevant. Success isn't about where you are now; it's about whether you're willing to learn, innovate, and embrace change. In today's fast-paced world, staying curious is your biggest asset.

Why These Stories?

You might be wondering, "Wasn't this chapter supposed to explain why you wrote this book?" Yes, it was but life doesn't follow a straight path, does it? Just like you might start a business and end up with more liabilities than assets, or start studying and end up sleeping through your classes. Life is unpredictable.

You might think that "Why start with negativity? I bought this book to feel motivated, not frustrated!" Relax, no more doom and gloom I promise.

Because life can also surprise you in amazing ways. You might start a business and end up a billionaire. Or start studying and graduate at the top of your class. That's the beauty of doing. Action creates outcomes, both good and bad.

Reading this book won't make you successful by itself. I'm not a social media "guru" who'll tell you to "Be a Sigma male/female" or "Go against the flow like an alpha." That's fluff. What matters is action.

You're already doing something important: reading this book. That's the first step. But the real power comes from what you do next.

So, why did I write this book? To remind you that progress isn't about flashy slogans or endless motivation. It's about the simple act of showing up, learning, failing, and growing.

Let's dive in and see how far you can go.

The world might admire your grades and titles at first, but in the long run, it's your ability to learn, adapt, and keep showing up that defines how far you'll go.

AM I EVEN QUALIFIED TO WRITE THIS BOOK?

Let's be real, who decides if someone is qualified to write a book? I'm not a scholar, and I don't have any fancy degrees to flash. What I do have, though, is experience, curiosity, and an unshakable passion for learning. Some of my friends call me a madman, and honestly, they're not entirely wrong. Why? Because I'm the type who dares to do things differently, refusing to just go with the flow.

My real qualification? The lessons I've learned through real-life experiences, insights from incredible books, and wisdom shared by like-minded people. I've stumbled, I've failed, and I've grown and now I'm here to share it all with you. Consider this book a guide, not from a master, but from someone who's been in the trenches, hoping to give you a heads-up on the road ahead.

1. **Grades Don't Define You:** I struggled in school, but that didn't stop me from creating valuable work in the real world.
2. **Experience Is the Best Teacher:** You don't need a degree to be qualified, you need the courage to try and fail.
3. **Stay Curious:** The more you learn, the more doors open.

Grades Don't Define You:

At 15, I got hooked on geopolitics. While others were busy with games or social media, I was tracking global events, trying to understand how the world works. By 19, I had already started investing in the stock market and set up my SIPs. That same year,

I began posting regularly on LinkedIn, turning into a content creator. I wasn't just dabbling, I was committed.

Here's the twist: I was the guy who struggled to pass in school. I didn't get great grades. In fact, sometimes just passing felt like a victory. But that didn't stop me from learning outside the classroom.

Experience Is the Best Teacher:

By the time I turned 20, I landed an internship with ATIUM Sports, a startup focused on sports science. My job? To create a Knowledge Repository a guide on how to use our platform effectively. Imagine that: the guy who struggled in school was now writing important documentation for a growing company. Later, I was given another big task developing the SOP (Standard Operating Procedure) for our second product, ATIUM AssessPro. These weren't small jobs, and yet, I took them head-on, even without a background in writing.

Stay Curious:

I'm not a professional writer, and I'm not trying to be one. I write because I love it. I started this book on April 9, 2024, at 10:35 PM, and within 20 minutes, I finished the first draft of the chapter "The Power of Fear." Why so fast? Because I've lived what I write about.

This book isn't about perfection, it's about sharing real experiences. It's packed with honesty, humor, and insights. You'll find a bit of madness in every chapter, but if you take it seriously, it might just change the way you see the world.

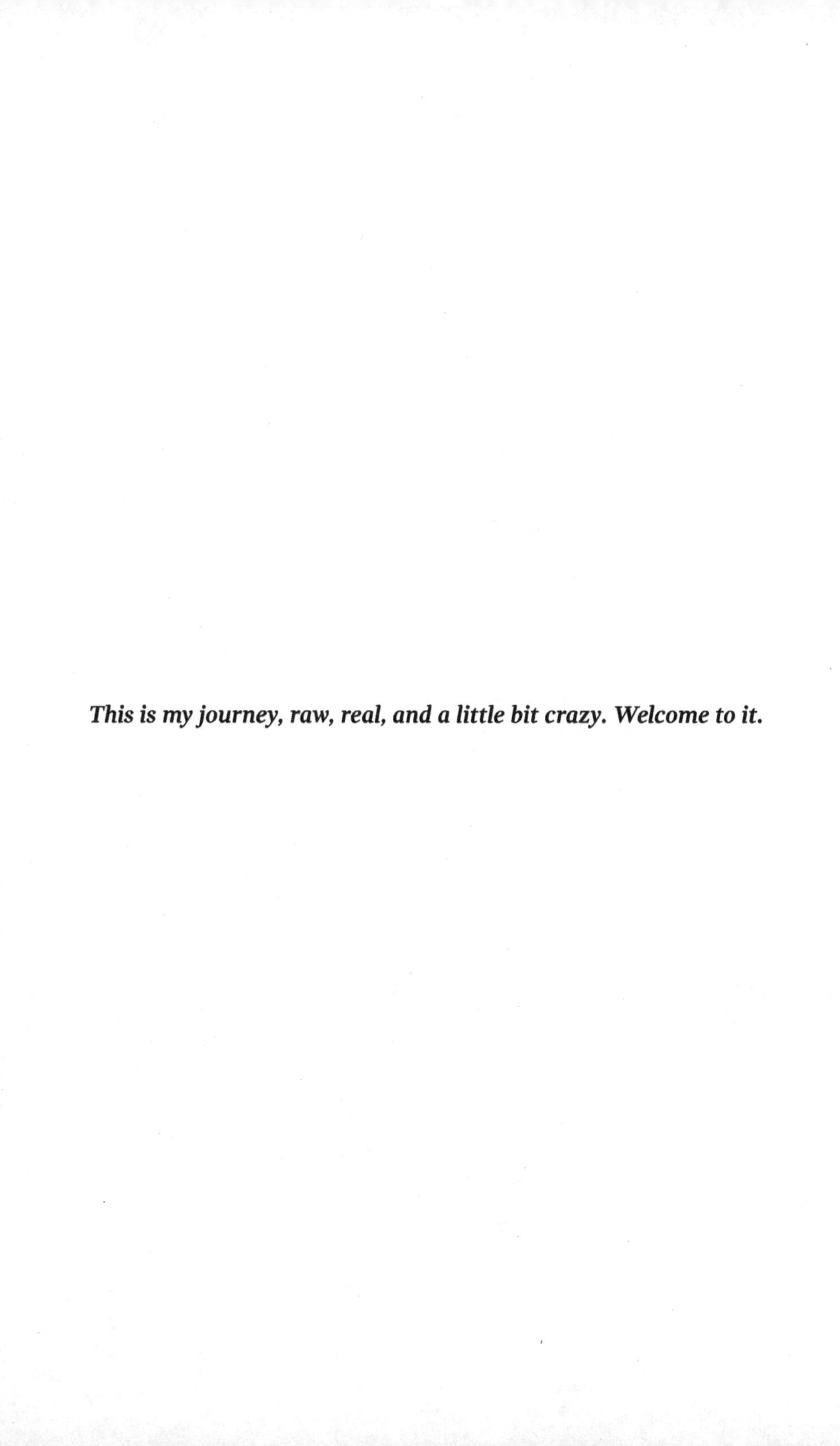

This is my journey, raw, real, and a little bit crazy. Welcome to it.

The Essential Powers For Growth

Cravings are the fuel, the direction you point them in determines whether they burn you out or build you up.

CHAPTER 1

POWER OF CRAVINGS

What are cravings? It's that pull you feel when you see a new movie trailer and can't wait to watch it. It's the urge to eat your favorite food when you just think about it. Cravings are powerful because they drive immediate, undeniable action. Now imagine if you redirected that energy into something bigger, something that could change your life.

Cravings push you to consume something right away, but what if you craved success? What if you hungered for progress so deeply that you couldn't sit still until you achieved it? That's the secret. Instead of procrastinating, you'd dive into productive work to satisfy that craving. The more you crave something positive, the more effort you'll put into it. Over time, those efforts compound, and you'll find yourself far ahead of where you used to be.

I'm not sharing this just for the sake of it. I personally experienced the power of cravings in my life. Craving success is what got me here, writing this book. It's what stopped me from wasting time on distractions and entertainment. In my career, I shine in my field because I craved recognition not empty praise, but the kind that comes from delivering real results.

As I mentioned prior when I joined as an intern in February 2024, I had my hands full with two final-year projects, assignments, and exams. My friends told me to take it easy, to give up on content creation because it wasn't worth the stress. But I craved recognition from my CEO. I wanted to prove my worth. I worked late nights, often till midnight, just to meet deadlines and deliver quality work.

By the end of my three-month internship, I was offered the position of Relationship Manager.

If I hadn't craved recognition, I wouldn't be where I am today. Cravings, when channeled correctly, can push you to achieve more than you thought possible. If it worked for me, why not for you?

The Man Who Never Stopped Craving

Imagine this: You've worked hard, spent a ton of money, and built something you believe in. Then BOOM! It fails. Not once, not twice, but three times. Most people would quit and never look back. But not Elon Musk. Why? Because he craved something more.

Elon Musk wanted rockets that didn't just go to space. He wanted them to come back and land safely so they could be used again. Sounds simple now, but back then, it was nearly impossible. Every time a rocket exploded, people laughed at him. Critics said it would never work. Investors were ready to pull out. But Musk didn't stop. He kept going because his craving for success was stronger than his fear of failure.

After years of hard work and many sleepless nights, SpaceX finally succeeded. In 2008, the Falcon 1 rocket became the first privately-built rocket to reach space. It was a huge moment, but did Musk stop there? No. He kept craving more.

He worked even harder to make rockets reusable. People thought he was crazy, but now SpaceX rockets land back on Earth like it's the most normal thing ever. Musk didn't stop there either. He started working on making life on Mars possible. Why? Because he craves to achieve what no one else even dreams of.

Today, Elon Musk is the richest man in the world, with a net worth of over $400 billion. But it's not just about the money. It's about the fact that he never stops craving the next big thing.

The lesson: If you crave something big, don't stop until you get it. And when you do, crave the next step. That's how you grow. If Musk can turn his cravings into rockets that touch the stars, what can you do with yours?

Human Psychology Behind Cravings

Let's dig deeper into why cravings have such a powerful impact on our actions and how understanding them can change the game. To make it clear, let's revisit Elon Musk's story.

When Musk started SpaceX, he wasn't just building rockets; he was satisfying a deep craving, a craving to revolutionize space exploration and prove reusable rockets were possible. That craving wasn't born overnight. It grew from his passion for innovation, his fear of stagnation, and his insatiable curiosity.

Here's how psychology explains it:

1. **Cravings are rooted in dopamine:**
   When you set a goal or desire something, your brain releases dopamine—the "feel-good" chemical. It's this surge of dopamine that pushes you to act, to work hard, and to overcome challenges. For Musk, every step closer to a successful rocket launch likely triggered a dopamine rush, fueling his next move.
2. **Anticipation creates momentum:**
   Cravings are strongest when the outcome feels achievable but not yet reached. Musk faced numerous failures, rockets that exploded, critics who doubted him but the anticipation of success kept him going. That's the magic of cravings: they thrive on the "almost there" feeling.
3. **Fear and craving work together:**
   Musk wasn't just driven by his desire for success; he was also motivated by the fear of failure. This combination of craving and fear creates an unstoppable force. The fear of giving up or being proven wrong amplified his craving to succeed, making him relentless.
4. **Cravings are contagious:**
   When you crave something passionately, it inspires others to join you. Musk's vision for SpaceX wasn't just his own; it resonated with his team, investors, and even the public. His craving became a shared mission, driving collective effort.

So, what's the lesson here? Cravings aren't just fleeting desires; they're deeply wired into our psychology. If you channel them correctly, like Musk did, they can become a force that drives you toward extraordinary results.

Think of your cravings as fuel.
Are you using them to propel yourself forward,
or are they burning you out?

Fearlessness may make you bold,
but essential fear makes you unstoppable.

CHAPTER 2

THE POWER OF FEAR

Fear. The very word often gets a bad rap. Society tells us to be fearless, to conquer fear as if it's some villain holding us back. But let's pause for a moment. Is being completely fearless really the answer? Or is fear, when used wisely, actually a hidden strength?

Let me tell you about two people from the same district but on completely different paths Jacob, the so-called "fearless," and Saha, who discovered the real power of essential fear.

The Danger of Being Fearless

Jacob was the kind of guy who could light up a room with his carefree attitude. Born and raised in Kanyakumari, he was the life of the party, the joker among his friends, and the one who always had a shrug for life's challenges. His motto? "Why worry about tomorrow when today is here to enjoy?"

At first, his fearlessness seemed like a gift. While others stressed over exams, Jacob was chilling, playing video games late into the night. When his friends worried about backlogs, Jacob waved it off, saying, "Life is too short to stress over marks."

But life has a funny way of showing us the consequences of our choices.

By the end of his second year in college, Jacob had accumulated a staggering two-digit number of arrears. He didn't care about lectures, assignments, or even exams. While his friends were securing internships, Jacob was busy chasing the next level in a video game or planning his next hangout.

His parents, seeing his carefree attitude, were deeply worried. They tried reasoning with him, warning him of the future.

His friends, too, encouraged him to take life seriously. But Jacob laughed it all off, proudly declaring, "Why should I fear failure? Fear is for the weak."

But here's the twist: Jacob's fearlessness wasn't making him a hero. It was making him stagnant.

The Impact of Fearlessness

Fearlessness sounds great on motivational posters, but in reality, it often leads to complacency. Jacob wasn't afraid of failure, but that wasn't because he was strong, it was because he didn't care.

No fear of failure: This meant no drive to improve. Why bother studying when he wasn't afraid of failing the exam?

No fear of consequences: He didn't worry about his future. He wasn't concerned about the job market or his skills.

No fear of accountability: He dismissed his parents' concerns and ignored the advice of his friends.

Fearlessness had turned into carelessness. Jacob's life became a cycle of missed opportunities, wasted time, and unfulfilled potential. His so-called bravery wasn't helping him grow; it was keeping him stuck.

The Lesson

Fear isn't the enemy, it's the spark that keeps us on our toes, the voice that pushes us to prepare and grow. Jacob's story shows us what happens when fear is completely absent: a life with no direction, no progress, and no purpose.

Fearlessness may sound inspiring, but without responsibility and ambition, it can lead to failure, not the kind we learn from, but the kind we regret.

So ask yourself: Are you being fearless, or are you avoiding the essential fears that could drive you toward success?

How Fear Became Fuel

In the quiet town of Colachel, nestled in the Kanyakumari district, lived a girl named Saha. Unlike Jacob, Saha wasn't known for being carefree or fearless. In fact, she was quite the opposite. Saha was deeply aware of her responsibilities, and with that awareness came a fair amount of fear, fear of failing, fear of disappointing her parents, and fear of an uncertain future.

But here's what made Saha different: she didn't let fear paralyze her. Instead, she used it to push herself forward.

Saha's mornings often started before sunrise. While others were still snoozing or scrolling through their phones, Saha was at her desk, flipping through her textbooks. Her friends would ask, "Why do you stress so much? Relax a little!" But for Saha, the stakes were too high to take it easy.

The Fear That Drove Her

Saha's fears weren't the kind that made her anxious or defeated. They were the kind that kept her grounded and focused.

Fear of letting her parents down: Saha came from a modest family. Her parents had worked hard to provide for her education, and she feared wasting their sacrifices.

Fear of missed opportunities: She knew the world was competitive. If she didn't study, someone else would take the opportunities meant for her.

Fear of failure: This wasn't a crippling fear. Instead, it was a question she asked herself every day: If I don't prepare now, how will I face tomorrow?

When her friends called her out for being "too serious," she would laugh and say, "I'd rather stress a little now than regret a lot later."

How Saha Used Fear

One night, during exam season, Saha found herself overwhelmed. Procrastination whispered, "Just take a break. Watch some TV." But as soon as she thought of how unprepared she would feel in the exam hall, that essential fear kicked in. She snapped out of it, picked up her pen, and kept studying.

When others gave up on difficult subjects, Saha tackled them head-on.

While her friends pulled all-nighters before exams, Saha was consistent, studying a little every day.

When results came out, she didn't just pass, she excelled.

The Payoff

Saha's story didn't end with just good grades. That essential fear drove her to plan her future with precision.

- She secured a scholarship to a top university.
- She got placed in a reputable company with a salary that her parents could only dream of.
- Most importantly, she proved to herself that fear, when embraced, could be a powerful ally.

The Lesson

Saha's fear didn't make her weak; it made her unstoppable. It wasn't the type of fear that froze her in place, it was the kind that reminded her of what was at stake.

If Saha had been fearless like Jacob, she might have dismissed her responsibilities. Instead, she used her fears as a guiding compass, steering her toward a better future.

Fear vs. Essential Fear

Fear is often misunderstood. Many see it as a negative emotion, something to be avoided or eliminated. But is all fear truly bad? If you've followed Jacob and Saha's stories, you might already sense where this is going. Let's take another look at their experiences to clearly see the difference between fear and essential fear.

Jacob prided himself on being fearless. But his version of fearlessness wasn't empowering, it was destructive.

- Jacob didn't fear failure, so he didn't care about his arrears.
- He didn't fear the consequences of his actions, so he wasted his time.

- He didn't fear disappointing his family, so he ignored their concerns.

Without any fear to ground him, Jacob became complacent. Fearlessness, in his case, wasn't a strength, it was a lack of accountability. It wasn't pushing him forward; it was holding him back.

Jacob's story shows that being fearless can lead to carelessness. Without fear, there's no urgency or motivation to act. His fearlessness didn't make him brave; it left him stuck.

On the other hand, Saha didn't run away from fear; she embraced it. But her fear was different. It wasn't the kind that made her anxious or frozen. It was essential fear, the kind that motivated her to take action.

- She feared disappointing her parents, so she studied diligently.
- She feared failing, so she prepared consistently.
- She feared missing opportunities, so she stayed disciplined.

Saha's essential fear wasn't about avoiding consequences, it was about creating a better future. It kept her accountable and focused, driving her toward her goals.

Saha's story shows that essential fear is not a weakness, it's a catalyst. It pushes you out of your comfort zone and keeps you striving for growth.

The Key Differences

Fear	Essential Fear
Paralyses you	Motivates you
Makes you avoid challenges	Encourage you to face challenges
Leads to procrastination	Drives Consistent action

Why This Matters

Fear, in its raw form, can be a burden. But essential fear? That's a gift. The difference lies in how you channel it. Jacob's lack of fear made him careless, while Saha's essential fear made her unstoppable.

Think about your own fears:

Are they holding you back like Jacob's?

Or are they driving you forward like Saha's?

By understanding and embracing essential fear, you can turn what seems like a weakness into one of your greatest strengths. Don't aim to be fearless, aim to harness the power of fear to fuel your growth.

The Science Behind Fear and Essential Fear

Fear isn't just an emotion it's a survival tool. Your brain has been hardwired to respond to threats, ensuring you survive in dangerous situations. But not all fear is created equal. Understanding the science behind fear and how it transforms into essential fear can help us harness its power for growth.

The Amygdala:

Fear starts in the amygdala, the part of your brain responsible for processing emotions. When you sense danger, the amygdala sends an alarm signal.

The Fight-or-Flight Response:

Your body reacts by releasing stress hormones like adrenaline and cortisol. These hormones.

- Increase your heart rate.
- Heighten your senses.
- Prepare your muscles for action.

This response was crucial when humans faced physical dangers like wild animals. But in modern life, fear often comes from less tangible threats, like failure, rejection, or uncertainty.

Fear vs. Essential Fear: What's the Difference?

The key difference lies in how your brain interprets fear.

1. **Fear (Uncontrolled):**
   - Causes overthinking and paralysis.

- Triggers the "freeze" response, making you avoid challenges.
- Keeps you stuck in a state of anxiety.

2. Essential Fear (Controlled):

- Activates the prefrontal cortex, the rational part of your brain.
- Helps you assess risks and take constructive action.
- Drives you to prepare, plan, and improve.

Essential fear transforms the raw, panicked response of the amygdala into a calculated, productive approach through logical thinking.

The Role of Dopamine

Dopamine, the "feel-good" chemical in your brain, plays a significant role in how fear can become a motivating force.

When you overcome a challenge or move closer to a goal, your brain releases dopamine.

This creates a positive feedback loop:

Fear motivates action → Action leads to success → Success releases dopamine → You crave more progress.

In Saha's case:

Her fear of failure drove her to study.

Each small win, like completing a topic or passing an exam, released dopamine.

This kept her motivated to achieve even more.

In Jacob's case:

His lack of fear meant no urgency, no action, and no dopamine rewards.

Why Fear is Essential for Growth

Fear, when used correctly, can be your brain's way of saying, "This matters!"

It sharpens your focus.

It pushes you out of your comfort zone.

It keeps you accountable to your goals.

Don't let fear control you. Instead, channel it into essential fear as a tool for preparation, discipline, and persistence.

Simple Analogy: Fear is Like Fire

Uncontrolled fear (fire) can burn you and destroy everything around you.

Controlled fear (fire) can cook your food, keep you warm, and light your path.

It's not about eliminating fear, it's about learning to control and use it effectively.

Fear isn't your enemy.
It's a tool your brain gives you to push forward.
By understanding how fear works and channeling
it as essential fear, you can turn anxiety into action,
uncertainty into confidence, and hesitation into growth.

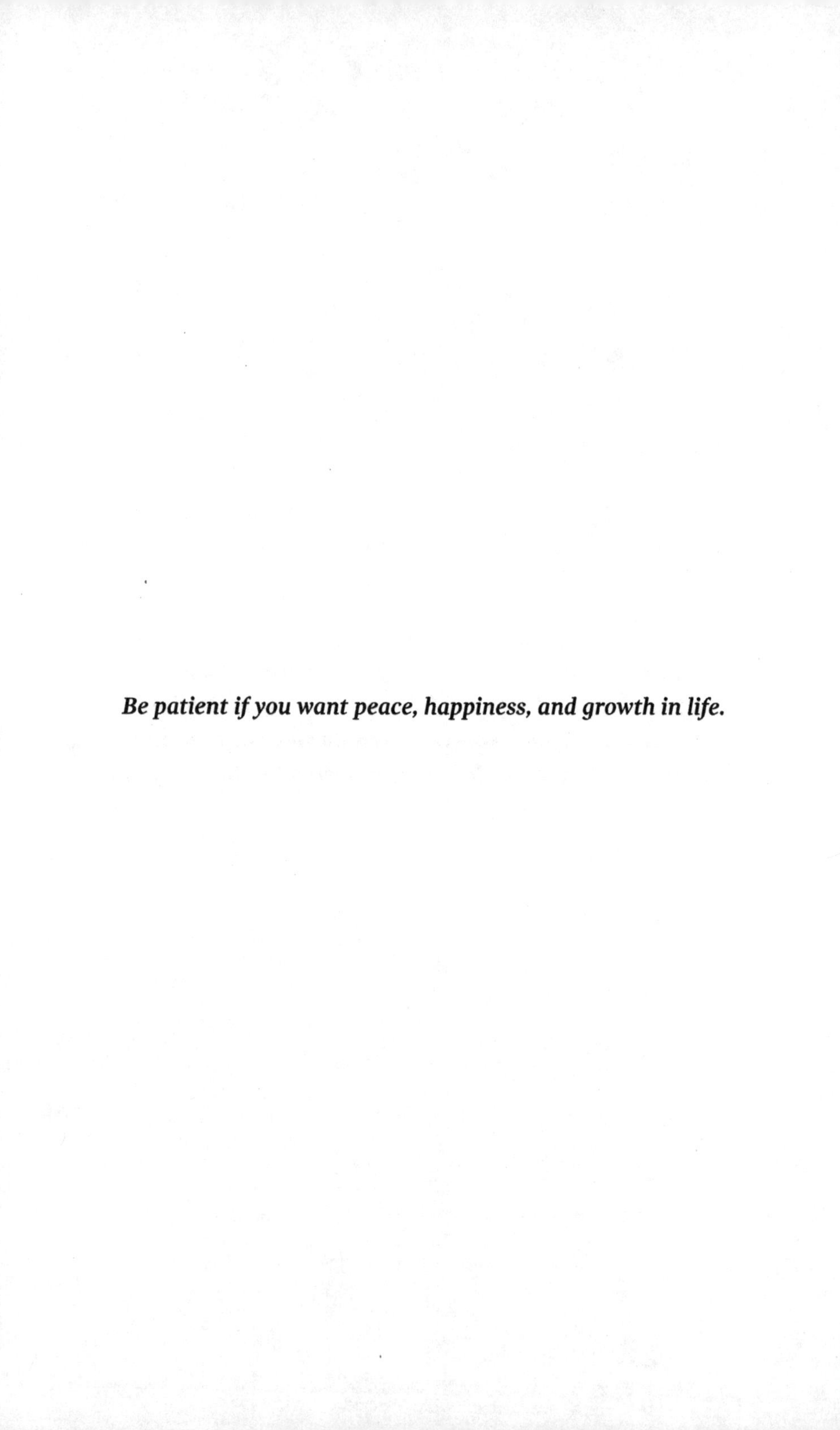

Be patient if you want peace, happiness, and growth in life.

CHAPTER 3

THE POWER OF PATIENCE

Patience. It's something we've all heard about but rarely practice. Remember when you ordered biryani and had to wait while the aroma filled the room? Or the time you stood in line at your favorite parotta stall, watching others get served before you? That's patience right there. It's frustrating, isn't it? But when the plate finally lands in front of you, the taste feels sweeter, like it was worth the wait.

Life works the same way. The best things are success, growth, or even a better tomorrow that takes time. But in a world where everything happens fast, like instant noodles or one-click shopping, waiting feels like a punishment. We want results now, whether it's getting fit, learning a skill, or seeing our efforts pay off.

Yet, think about it. Would you expect a seed to grow into a tree the next day? No. You water it, give it sunlight, and wait. Slowly, it grows. The same applies to life. Patience is not just sitting idle, it's about trusting the process, staying consistent, and believing that your hard work will pay off eventually.

We've all mocked someone for saying, "Be patient." Maybe we called them "Boomer" or "Aunty." But deep down, there's wisdom in their words. Whether it's your mom telling you to wait for biryani to cook or a mentor advising you to trust the journey, they've lived enough to know that rushing things rarely leads to anything good.

Patience isn't boring. It's powerful. It's the secret ingredient that makes success last. Think of the people you admire. They didn't achieve great things overnight. They worked, waited, and kept going when nothing seemed to happen.

In this chapter, we'll dive into why patience matters. We'll explore how it helps you face challenges, stay focused, and build something meaningful. Whether it's waiting for parotta or your dreams, patience is the skill that makes the wait worthwhile. And trust me, it's always worth it in the end.

The Cost of Impatience

Kannan and Divya were deeply in love, despite the distance between them. Kannan lived in Pondicherry, while Divya was in North India. They talked for hours every day, their conversations filled with laughter and dreams.

One day, during the Holi festival, Kannan texted Divya

Kannan: "Babe, I know today is Holi. You'll be celebrating with your friends. I won't text until the evening. Enjoy your day! Love you."

Divya: "Okay, see you in the evening!"

Feeling extra affectionate, Kannan added: "Miss you." But to his surprise, Divya didn't reply.

At first, Kannan brushed it off, thinking she was busy with the celebrations. But as time passed, his mind started racing. By afternoon, he decided to open Instagram, and what he saw hit him like a punch to the gut.

Divya was posting stories laughing, throwing colors, and having a great time. Yet, his message sat unread.

Frustration boiled over. He checked his phone every few minutes, hoping for a response, but nothing came. Thoughts consumed him: Is she ignoring me? Has she forgotten about me?

By evening, Divya finally texted, sending cheerful pictures of her day.

Divya: "It was such a fun day, Kannan! Hope you're doing well. Love you!"

But instead of appreciating her effort, Kannan let his frustration spill out.

Kannan: "Why didn't you check my message? You were online the whole day but didn't even think about me. Am I not important to you anymore?"

Divya was stunned. She replied hesitantly:

Divya: "Kannan, I was just using Instagram filters for pictures. My friends posted the stories. You told me to enjoy my day, so I thought it was okay."

Kannan froze. He realized she hadn't ignored him; she was simply doing what he had promised to let her do: enjoy her day. But his impatience had already hurt her.

Feeling guilty, Kannan called Divya and apologized profusely.

Kannan: "I'm sorry, Divya. I overreacted. I let my emotions get the better of me. You didn't deserve that."

Divya forgave him, but their relationship wasn't the same. Over the next few weeks, Kannan noticed Divya growing distant. One evening, she finally opened up.

Divya: "Kannan, I love you, but your lack of trust and patience makes me question if this relationship can work. I need someone who believes in me, even in the small things."

Her words shattered him. His impatience had done more damage than he realized.

Months later, they drifted apart. Kannan was left with regret for a lesson learned too late. He realized that patience isn't just about waiting; it's about trusting, listening, and allowing space for the people we care about.

Got it! Here's how we can structure it:

The Cost of Patience

In Kannan and Divya's story, we saw why patience is vital in relationships and how rushing emotions can harm what we hold dear. Now, let's explore why patience is equally crucial for development, be it physical, mental, or professional growth. And who better to illustrate this than Arnold Schwarzenegger, a global icon known for his incredible journey of transforming himself from a small-town boy in Austria to a bodybuilding legend, Hollywood superstar, and political leader.

The Early Days of Arnold

Arnold didn't wake up one day with a chiseled body or worldwide fame. His story started in a small village in Austria, where he had a clear dream: to become the best bodybuilder in the world. But the path to this dream wasn't smooth. He wasn't born with a muscular physique, nor did he have access to high-tech gyms. What he did have was an unshakable belief in his vision and the patience to put in the work.

Every day, Arnold followed a rigorous training schedule. He would lift heavy weights, train for hours, and push himself beyond his limits. But building muscle doesn't happen overnight. It's a slow process that requires consistency, proper nutrition, and, above all, patience.

The Power of Patience in Bodybuilding

Muscle growth, scientifically known as hypertrophy, is a gradual process. When you work out, you create tiny tears in your muscle fibers. These tears heal and grow stronger over time, but it's a process that takes weeks, months, and even years. Arnold understood this deeply. He didn't get discouraged when he didn't see immediate results. Instead, he focused on the small improvements: an extra rep, a heavier weight, or slightly better form.

Arnold once said, "The last three or four reps are what makes the muscle grow. This area of pain divides the champion from someone who is not a champion." His patience allowed him to endure the pain, wait for the results, and keep going when others gave up.

The Long Road to Success

Arnold didn't just win one or two titles he became a seven-time Mr. Olympia champion. But even after achieving his dream in bodybuilding, his patience didn't end there. Transitioning into acting, he faced rejection after rejection. Directors said his accent was too strong, his body too big for traditional roles. Yet Arnold didn't lose hope. He took his time, worked on his skills, and eventually landed iconic roles in movies like The Terminator and Conan the Barbarian.

Why This Story Matters

Arnold's journey shows us that patience is not about waiting idly, it's about putting in the effort every single day, even when the results seem far away. Whether you're building muscle, developing a career, or learning a new skill, success is a gradual process.

Just like in bodybuilding, the small, consistent actions you take day after day will eventually compound into something extraordinary. Impatience leads to burnout or quitting, but patience keeps you in the game long enough to achieve greatness.

If Kannan and Divya's story showed us the importance of patience in relationships, Arnold's story teaches us the importance of patience in building ourselves. Whether it's muscle, a career, or a legacy, the key is to keep going, trust the process, and give it time.

Your personal brand is your story.
Own it, live it, and tell it to the world.
If you consistently provide value,
opportunities will find their way to you.

CHAPTER 4

The Power Personal Branding

Imagine this: You walk into a room full of people, and someone instantly recognizes you not for how you look, but for the value you bring. They know your story, your expertise, and your unique edge. That's the magic of personal branding.

Personal branding isn't just for celebrities or influencers. It's for anyone who wants to stand out in today's noisy world. Whether you're a student, a professional, an entrepreneur, or even a freelancer, your personal brand is your identity, it's how people perceive you and what you stand for.

Why Personal Branding is Important

1. **Visibility and Recognition**
   In today's competitive world, it's not just about what you know or what you do, it's about how people remember you. A strong personal brand ensures you're seen and remembered for the right reasons, making opportunities find you.
2. **Building Trust**
   People trust individuals, not faceless organizations. When you build a personal brand, you're creating a reputation that speaks for you. It's your promise of consistency, credibility, and authenticity.

3. **Opportunities Knock on Your Door**
   A well-crafted personal brand can open doors to collaborations, job offers, and partnerships. It positions you as a thought leader in your field, making others seek your advice or services.
4. **Control Your Narrative**
   If you don't define who you are, someone else will. Personal branding allows you to take charge of your story, highlight your strengths, and shape how the world sees you.
5. **Helps in Career Growth**
   Whether you're climbing the corporate ladder or starting your own venture, your personal brand showcases your expertise, differentiating you from the competition and fast-tracking your growth.

The Foundation of a Personal Brand

Think of your personal brand as your digital and real-world resume. It's built through:

- Your actions: What you consistently deliver.
- Your communication: What you say and how you say it.
- Your network: Who you connect with and how you add value to them.
- Your presence: How you appear online and offline.

In the chapters ahead, we'll explore how personal branding has transformed the lives of ordinary people into extraordinary success stories, how to build one effectively, and how patience and persistence like in previous chapters play a crucial role in sustaining it.

How to build your personal brand

Personal branding isn't about spending loads of money on certifications or taking dozens of courses. Sure, those things help, but they're not the core of building a powerful brand. What truly matters is how you present yourself and consistently add value. It's about showing the world who you are, what you stand for, and why you're worth paying attention to.

Think of personal branding as a reflection of your authentic self. Fancy titles or polished resumes might get you noticed, but your impact is determined by how well you connect with others and how you showcase your skills, ideas, and values.How You Present Yourself Offline and Online.

Personal branding starts the moment you interact with someone be it face-to-face or in the digital world. Let's break it down:

Offline Presence

Your offline interactions are just as crucial as your online ones. Think about:

Your body language: A confident handshake, eye contact, and a genuine smile can say a lot about you before you even speak.

How you communicate: The words you choose and the way you speak reflect your mindset and attitude. Listening actively is as important as speaking clearly.

The value you bring: Whether in a meeting, a classroom, or a casual gathering, share ideas, offer help, and leave people better than you found them.

Consistency is key. If you're helpful, approachable, and authentic offline, people will naturally gravitate toward you, forming a solid foundation for your personal brand.

Online Presence

Your online presence is your 24/7 resume. Even when you're not actively networking, your profiles, posts, and interactions speak for you.

1. **Professional Profiles**
   Optimize your LinkedIn profile with a professional photo, a headline that defines your niche, and a summary that highlights your unique skills and achievements.
   Keep your bio clean and consistent across platforms like Instagram, Twitter, or any other platform you use.
2. **Content Creation**
   Share your expertise through blogs, articles, videos, or posts. Whether it's insights from your industry, lessons

from your life, or your perspective on current events, people will associate you with your knowledge.
Post consistently. Even if you're starting small, showing up regularly builds trust over time.

3. **Engagement**
   Don't just post. Reply to comments, participate in discussions, and connect with others in your field. It shows you're approachable and willing to add value.
4. **Portfolio Showcase**
   Use platforms like Behance, GitHub, or even a personal website to showcase your work. Whether you're a designer, developer, writer, or marketer, having an accessible portfolio sets you apart.

Once your offline and online foundation is set, the next step is to expand your reach.

1. **Collaborate**
   Partner with others in your field. This could mean co-writing articles, appearing on podcasts, or contributing to projects. Collaboration exposes you to a wider audience.
2. **Network Intelligently**
   Attend webinars, join forums, and engage in industry-specific groups online. These spaces are filled with like-minded people who can offer insights and opportunities.
   Don't hesitate to send a meaningful connection request on LinkedIn or a thoughtful DM on Instagram.
3. **Stay Consistent**
   Your personal brand isn't built overnight. Stick to your core message, keep delivering value, and remain consistent in your efforts. People trust those who show up regularly.
4. **Leverage Social Media Algorithms**
   Platforms like LinkedIn and Instagram reward active users. Use hashtags, optimize post timings, and keep experimenting with different content formats text posts, carousels, videos, etc.

5. **Learn and Adapt**
   Personal branding isn't static. Pay attention to what works and what doesn't. Adapt your strategies based on feedback and analytics.

Why It Matters

Personal branding is your long-term investment in yourself. The more effort you put into presenting your authentic self, the more opportunities you'll create. In the next section, we'll dive into the inspiring story of an individual who turned ordinary beginnings into extraordinary success through personal branding.

The Story of Superstar Rajinikanth: How Personal Branding Changed His Life

Let's take a look at one of the most inspiring stories in Indian cinema: the rise of Superstar Rajinikanth. Today, he's a global icon, but his journey is a testament to how personal branding, even without the fancy labels, can open doors and change lives.

Before he became Rajinikanth, the superstar, he was Shivaji Rao Gaekwad, a regular man from a modest background. Born in Bangalore, he worked as a bus conductor for Bangalore Transport Service.

Even in this role, Shivaji stood out. How? It wasn't about his uniform or job, it was his style. His unique way of issuing tickets, flipping coins, and interacting with passengers became his trademark. People loved his charisma and energy. Some even took the bus just to watch him in action. Without knowing it, Shivaji was building a personal brand: the stylish, confident man with a larger-than-life personality.

Shivaji's life took a dramatic turn when he joined the Madras Film Institute to study acting. He wasn't the typical hero material; he didn't fit the image of tall, fair-skinned leads who dominated cinema. But what he had was his unique identity and his style.

Director K. Balachander, one of Tamil cinema's legends, noticed Shivaji during a stage performance. Balachander didn't see just another aspiring actor; he saw a man with a magnetic personality. Shivaji's on-stage presence, dialogue delivery, and mannerisms left a lasting impression.

Balachander gave him his first break in Tamil cinema with a small role in the movie Apoorva Raagangal (1975). He even advised Shivaji to adopt the screen name "Rajinikanth," and the rest is history.

Why Style Became His Brand

Rajinikanth didn't try to copy anyone. Instead, he embraced what made him unique: his unconventional looks, his rapid-fire dialogue delivery, and, most importantly, his style. From flipping cigarettes to his signature walk, everything about him screamed originality.

This authenticity resonated with audiences. People didn't just watch his movies; they celebrated them. His style became his personal brand, and it turned him into a cultural phenomenon. Even decades later, fans around the world mimic his iconic gestures and dialogue delivery.

The Lesson

Rajinikanth's journey teaches us that personal branding isn't about fitting into a mold, it's about standing out. He didn't need a fancy education, expensive clothes, or an influential network. He simply amplified what made him him.

In the same way, your personal brand is built on your unique qualities, skills, and personality. Whether you're a bus conductor, a student, or an entrepreneur, how you present yourself both offline and online matters.

Rajinikanth's style wasn't just his flair; it was his ticket to success. And that's the power of personal branding: when done right, it can take you from ordinary to extraordinary.

LIFE'S CORE PRINCIPLES

Motivation is a spark,
but consistency is the engine that takes you to your destination.

CHAPTER 5

Consistency Over Motivation

Motivation feels great, doesn't it? It's that rush of energy you get after watching an inspiring video or hearing a powerful speech. You feel unstoppable, ready to conquer your goals. But let's be real, how long does that feeling last? A day? A week? Maybe a month if you're lucky?

Motivation is like a spark; it ignites quickly but fades just as fast. On the other hand, consistency is the steady flame that keeps burning, no matter the weather. It's the habit of showing up every day, even when you don't feel like it, even when no one's watching, and even when progress seems invisible.

Think about it: what's the difference between someone who goes to the gym only when they feel motivated and someone who goes no matter what? The first person might see some results, but the second will transform their entire life. That's the power of consistency; it's not about how you feel in the moment; it's about committing to the process, rain or shine.

In this chapter, we're not going to rely on feel-good pep talks. Instead, we'll dig into why consistency beats motivation every single time. From stories that illustrate its importance to practical tips for building consistent habits, you'll learn why showing up matters more than feeling inspired.

By the end, you'll see that success isn't built on fleeting moments of motivation. It's built on the quiet, unglamorous grind of consistency. Let's dive in.

Why Consistency Works

1. **Builds Discipline:**
   - Consistency trains your mind to act regardless of how you feel.
   - Over time, tasks become automatic, like brushing your teeth or tying your shoes.
2. **Creates Habits:**
   - Small, repeated actions compound into significant results.
   - For example, reading 10 pages daily adds up to over 3,600 pages in a year.
3. **Reduces Emotional Dependence:**
   - You don't rely on being in the "mood" to act.
   - Consistency keeps you moving forward even on bad days.
4. **Delivers Long-Term Results:**
   - Success is not about occasional bursts of effort; it's about steady progress.
   - Think of it like planting seeds: water them daily, and you'll see a garden grow.

Why Motivation Fails

1. **It's Temporary:**
   - Motivation often comes in waves. You feel pumped today but drained tomorrow.
   - It's not reliable for long-term goals.
2. **Driven by Emotion:**
   - Motivation is tied to how you feel in the moment.
   - On tough days, it's easy to skip important tasks because you "don't feel like it."
3. **Focuses on Instant Gratification:**
   - Motivation thrives on quick wins, but real progress often takes time.
   - When results aren't immediate, motivation fades.
4. **It's Situational:**

- Motivation is sparked by external triggers like inspiring videos or speeches.
- Once the trigger is gone, so is the drive to act.

By focusing on consistency, you build a system that doesn't rely on fleeting emotions, ensuring steady growth over time.

A Story of Consistency Over Motivation

MS Dhoni's journey from being a ticket collector in Kharagpur to becoming one of the most successful captains in cricket history is a testament to the power of consistency.

Before the world knew him as "Captain Cool," Dhoni was a young boy from Ranchi with a dream of playing cricket at the highest level. Coming from a small town with limited resources, Dhoni didn't have access to world-class facilities or coaches. But he had something more important: dedication and consistency.

Early Days of Struggle

Dhoni's days began at dawn, juggling school, football practice (his first love), and later cricket training.

To support his family, he worked as a ticket collector at the Kharagpur railway station. Despite the long hours and physically demanding work, Dhoni never skipped practice.

He didn't wait for motivation to strike. Whether he was tired, discouraged, or uncertain about his future, he showed up every day to work on his skills. His iconic helicopter shot? It didn't appear overnight,it was the result of countless hours of practice.

The Turning Point

In 2004, Dhoni got his break in the Indian cricket team. His debut was underwhelming, but he didn't let that shake him.

Over time, his consistency and calm mindset earned him recognition. By 2007, he was leading the Indian team to its first T20 World Cup victory.

Why Consistency Won

Unlike motivation, which comes and goes, Dhoni's focus on consistency kept him moving forward. He didn't rely on flashy moments or big speeches to stay on track. Instead, he believed in small, regular efforts—training, staying calm under pressure, and trusting the process.

Today, Dhoni is celebrated not just for his cricketing skills but for his unshakeable consistency, which helped India achieve historic milestones like winning the 2011 World Cup. His story teaches us that success isn't about being constantly motivated; it's about showing up, putting in the work, and trusting that the results will follow.

If it worked for Dhoni, if it worked for me, then why not for you? It's all up to you if you're ready to do the right thing consistently, it will pay off for sure.

Learning geopolitics won't make you a global leader overnight,
but it will make you a better thinker today

CHAPTER 6

WHY GEOPOLITICS?

The world we live in is more interconnected than ever before. Decisions made in one part of the globe ripple across economies, societies, and individual lives. Whether it's a diplomatic handshake, a trade agreement, or a military conflict, geopolitics is the thread that weaves together the global fabric. But why should it matter to you?

Understanding geopolitics isn't just for diplomats or policymakers. It equips everyday individuals with a deeper awareness of how the world functions, allowing you to anticipate changes, make informed decisions, and even find opportunities in chaos. Think of it like this: just as weather forecasts help you prepare for rain, monitoring geopolitics helps you navigate the global storms that affect markets, industries, and lives.

When I was in 10th standard, a random YouTube video changed everything for me. It was about India's nuclear ballistic missile variations, their tech, and their capabilities. I was awestruck. That single video ignited a craving in me to dive deeper and understand the world beyond what textbooks offered.

From that day, I began spending over five hours a day learning about war histories India's wars, World Wars I and II, the Berlin Wall, and the collapse of the USSR, etc. These stories opened my eyes to the interconnectedness of the world. Gradually, I shifted my focus to current global scenarios, what's happening and why it matters.

Geopolitics taught me how to think critically. Though not scientifically proven, I know the difference between the me before I became a geopolitics enthusiast and the me now.

It was my passion for geopolitics that indirectly led me to start investing in the stock market at the age of 19. Understanding global dynamics gave me the confidence to predict market trends and take calculated risks.

By 20, this passion even earned me recognition when my professor, Rinaldo De David, gave me the opportunity to present a talk on India's Agni-5 missile and MIRV technology in class. That moment was a milestone. It made me realize how far I had come just by following my curiosity.

How Geopolitics Shapes Us:

Geopolitics is more than a field of study; it's a lens through which we can view the world's interconnected systems. From wars and trade to technology and culture, geopolitics influences nearly every aspect of our lives. By understanding it, we unlock the potential to think globally, act strategically, and navigate life's complexities with clarity.

Here's how geopolitics can profoundly shape us:

1. **Expanded Thinking**
   Geopolitics forces us to think beyond our immediate surroundings and adopt a global perspective.
   For example, understanding why oil prices fluctuate isn't just about economics, it's tied to political tensions, trade routes, and international relations.
   When we follow global events, we start seeing how actions in one country can ripple across the world, influencing our daily lives.
   This expanded thinking enables us to approach personal and professional decisions with a broader, more informed mindset.
2. **Decision-Making Under Uncertainty**
   The world is unpredictable; wars, trade disputes, and natural disasters can change the global landscape in an instant.

Geopolitics teaches us how nations and leaders make decisions under uncertain circumstances.

Applying this skill helps us navigate personal challenges, like career changes or financial decisions, with greater confidence and adaptability.

3. **Connecting the Dots**

   Geopolitics reveals the interconnected nature of the world. For instance, a drought in one region might lead to global food shortages, driving inflation everywhere.

   Understanding these cause-and-effect relationships sharpens our analytical skills.

   This ability to connect dots isn't just useful in understanding global events, it's invaluable in business, investments, and personal planning.

4. **Strategic Thinking**

   Strategy is at the core of geopolitics, whether it's nations forming alliances or investing in specific industries.

   By studying these strategies, we learn to think ahead, anticipate challenges, and create opportunities.

   This mindset can be applied to personal goals, career growth, or entrepreneurial ventures, giving us a competitive edge.

5. **Economic Awareness**

   Global events often have direct economic impacts, from fluctuating oil prices to currency devaluations.

   Understanding these dynamics allows us to predict trends and make informed financial decisions, such as investments or savings plans.

   Whether you're an investor, a business owner, or an employee, staying geopolitically informed ensures you're better prepared for economic shifts.

6. **Technology Adoption**

   Geopolitics has always driven innovation.

   The space race between the U.S. and the Soviet Union, for instance, led to technological breakthroughs that still benefit us today.

By keeping an eye on global trends, like renewable energy or AI, we can adapt to new technologies early and leverage them for personal or professional growth.

7. **Seeing Multiple Sides**
   Geopolitics rarely presents a single truth—each nation has its own agenda and perspective.
   Learning to see multiple sides of an issue teaches empathy, critical thinking, and better decision-making.
   Whether it's understanding workplace dynamics or global conflicts, this skill equips us to handle situations with wisdom and balance.
8. **Cultural Awareness**
   Geopolitics opens doors to understanding diverse cultures, histories, and values.
   This fosters empathy and a global mindset, making us adaptable in multicultural environments.
   Whether in personal relationships or professional collaborations, cultural awareness enhances our ability to connect with others.
9. **Leadership Insights**
   Studying geopolitical scenarios shows us how leaders manage crises, negotiate, and make impactful decisions.
   These lessons inspire us to develop our leadership skills, helping us handle challenges in our own lives with poise and strategy.
10. **Adaptability to Change**
    The global landscape is constantly evolving, whether due to technological advancements or political shifts.
    Staying informed through geopolitics teaches us to embrace change and adjust our actions to new realities, be it a career shift or a societal transformation.

Start Now, It's Never Too Late

You may wonder if it's too late for you to start learning about geopolitics. Let me assure you it's not. The best time to start is now. Begin by following credible sources and watching multiple perspectives on the same news.

Don't trust a single media outlet. With media bias and propaganda being rampant, compare the same story across at least three different platforms to find the truth.

Risk isn't about gambling with your future, it's about stepping into the unknown to create one.

CHAPTER 7

WHY RISK?

Risk it's a word that often stirs up fear, hesitation, or doubt. Many of us associate it with uncertainty, failure, and loss. But here's the truth: every significant achievement, every breakthrough moment in history, every dream that turned into reality has one thing in common: someone, somewhere, took a risk.

Why? Because playing it safe might keep you comfortable, but it rarely leads to growth. Growth happens at the edge of your comfort zone, in the places where you challenge yourself, face uncertainty, and venture into the unknown. Risk is the bridge that connects where you are to where you want to be.

Think about it: every decision in life carries some level of risk. Starting a new job, entering a relationship, launching a business, or even pursuing a passion project all of these come with the possibility of failure. But they also carry the potential for incredible rewards, lessons, and transformations.

When you embrace risk, you unlock doors that would otherwise remain closed. You discover your strengths, uncover hidden opportunities, and build resilience. It's not about recklessness, it's about calculated risks, where you weigh the potential loss against the potential gain and make a choice to move forward despite the fear.

Why Should You Embrace Risk?

1. **Risk Builds Confidence**
   Taking risks, even small ones, proves to yourself that you're capable of facing challenges. Each step outside your comfort zone strengthens your belief in your abilities.

2. Risk Sparks Growth
   Staying in your comfort zone limits your potential. Taking risks pushes you to learn, adapt, and grow in ways you never thought possible.
3. **Risk Creates Opportunities**
   Many doors only open when you're willing to step into the unknown. Risk leads to opportunities that comfort could never provide.
4. **Risk Shapes Your Story**
   Your life's most memorable moments often come from the risks you took, the chances that scared you but ultimately shaped who you are.

In this chapter, we'll explore the mindset behind taking risks, the importance of calculated risk, and how to overcome the fear that holds you back. By the end, you'll see risk not as something to fear but as a tool for transformation.

In May 2024, I received a call from my CEO, Murugesh, asking me to come to Chennai for our second product demonstration and to write an SOP for our latest initiative. At that time, I was still interning remotely. Naturally, my mother was concerned traveling alone to an unfamiliar city felt unnecessary and risky to her. She wasn't wrong to worry. I had little experience navigating such situations independently, and I wasn't the adventurous type to begin with.

But something inside me told me this trip was important not just for the work itself but for what it could teach me. So, I decided to take the risk. I booked a bus, packed my essentials, and began my journey.

When I arrived in Chennai that morning, the city felt massive, unfamiliar, and a bit overwhelming. I spent the first half of the day figuring things out on my own. I booked a cab, found a hotel, and settled into the new environment. By noon, I met our CTO, Neelkanth, and that meeting changed everything.

Neelkanth didn't just welcome me to the team; he welcomed me into his life. From that day, he treated me like family. He provided me with accommodation, food, and most importantly, a sense of belonging. And what started as a temporary stay turned into something much bigger. I'm still here in Chennai, working as a core team member.

I know I've mentioned my internship several times in this book, but there's a reason for that: it genuinely changed my life. Every major lesson I've learned since then, every significant step I've taken, traces back to this phase of my journey.

Staying with Neelkanth was an experience in itself. He exposed me to the tech world in ways I hadn't imagined. We'd sit down for hours discussing backend processes, APIs, and the architecture of our software. His early career stories were incredibly inspiring, pushing me to work longer hours and approach challenges with a fresh perspective.

Beyond work, Neelkanth became a mentor who offered invaluable feedback not just about my technical skills but also about this very book. He pointed out areas where the content could be sharper, deeper, and more impactful. His feedback led me to rewrite and expand multiple chapters, adding 35% more content to intensify the core messages I wanted to share.

Why I Keep Coming Back to This Internship

It's simple: this internship wasn't just a professional milestone; it was a turning point in my life. It taught me to take risks, embrace discomfort, and trust the process. More importantly, it introduced me to people who believed in me and pushed me to grow.

When I left my comfort zone and came to Chennai, I didn't just find a new place to work; I found a new version of myself. And as I continue to live and work here, I see how that decision to take a risk has shaped who I am today.

Every chapter in this book has a lesson, and many of those lessons are tied to this pivotal experience. It's a story I keep referencing because it's a story that keeps giving me new insights. And if there's one thing I want you to take away from this, it's that stepping out of your comfort zone no matter how daunting can lead to opportunities and growth you never imagined.

So, yes, I'm still in Chennai, working hard as a core team member, learning and growing daily.

The Importance of Calculated Risks

Taking risks doesn't mean jumping blindly into uncertainty; it means making informed decisions where the potential rewards outweigh the possible setbacks. These are calculated risks, and they are essential for growth. Whether it's starting a new career, making an investment, or moving to a new city, calculated risks push us out of our comfort zones while keeping us grounded in reason.

Why are they important? Because nothing significant ever comes from playing it safe. Every breakthrough, personal or professional requires stepping into the unknown, but with preparation, strategy, and purpose.

Take my decision to go to Chennai as an example. It wasn't a random leap. I evaluated the opportunity, understood the challenges, and prepared myself to face them. Yes, there were risks: unfamiliarity, fear of failure, and the pressure of responsibility. But the rewards, a chance to grow, learn, and contribute outweighed them.

Overcoming the Fear That Holds You Back

Fear is the biggest barrier to taking risks. It whispers in your ear, "What if you fail?" or "What if it doesn't work out?" But here's the thing fear is often just a reflection of your imagination, not reality.

In the chapter on fear, we discussed how fear often feels like a giant shadow: intimidating, but baseless once confronted. The key is to break it down into manageable pieces.

Acknowledge It: Accept that fear is natural. It's your mind's way of protecting you from the unknown.

Analyze It: What exactly are you afraid of? Is it rejection, failure, or loss? Understand the root cause.

Prepare for It: Equip yourself with knowledge, skills, and resources. Preparation makes fear seem smaller and less overwhelming.

Act Despite It: Fear never fully goes away, but courage grows stronger when you take action in its presence.

Calculated risks and overcoming fear go hand in hand. When you calculate a risk, you focus on what's within your control. When you confront your fear, you prove to yourself that you're capable of more than you think.

If I had let fear hold me back, I wouldn't have taken the trip to Chennai, met mentors like Neelkanth and Murugesh, or grown into the person I am today. Fear doesn't mean stop; it means pause, evaluate, and move forward with intention.

So, the next time fear tries to hold you back, ask yourself:

"What's the worst that could happen? And am I prepared to handle it?" Chances are, the answer will embolden you to take that leap and it just might change your life.

Hobbies aren't just pastimes;
they're the building blocks of a unique identity.

CHAPTER 8

WHY HOBBIES?

Hobbies are not just pastimes; they are reflections of who we are, what we value, and how we see the world. They shape our personalities, enrich our experiences, and often reveal our true passions. While many view hobbies as secondary to skills or qualifications, they can be the very things that set you apart in a competitive world.

In a world where everyone is rushing to master professional skills, hobbies provide a breath of authenticity. They show your willingness to explore, your dedication to learning, and your ability to commit to something purely out of interest. Whether it's a unique interest like geopolitics or a common pursuit like fitness, hobbies often give you an edge, offering insights and abilities that formal education might overlook.

More than that, hobbies are a gateway to understanding yourself better. They teach you patience, focus, and a deeper sense of purpose. Whether you're preparing for an interview, writing a book, or simply navigating life, hobbies remind you that there's more to success than ticking boxes. They remind you to follow what excites you.

It was my final semester in college, and campus placements were announced. Like everyone else, I decided to give it a try. But here's the twist: I only got around to updating my resume at midnight before the interview.

When I finally looked at it, something caught my attention. My hobbies section had more points than my skills section. I couldn't help but laugh at myself. "Well, this is going to be interesting," I thought. I had no expectations of getting selected, but I figured the interview would at least be good practice.

The next morning, I walked into the interview room, handed over my resume, and waited. The HR glanced through it but didn't seem interested in my skills. Instead, her eyes landed on my hobbies section. She looked at me and asked, "What do you mean by geopolitics?"

I took a deep breath and started explaining. I used two examples making headlines at the time: the Russia-Ukraine war and the Israel-Palestine conflict. I explained how these events, even though far away, could affect things like global trade and fuel prices in India. For five minutes, I spoke passionately about what I had learned by following geopolitics over the years.

When I finished, she smiled and said, "You're in." That's how I got my first job offer because of my hobby.

Why Hobbies Matter

You might be wondering, Why is this story about hobbies? Here's the thing: I'm not a diplomat or an expert, but my hobby made me stand out.

Hobbies are more than just a way to pass time. They show who you are beyond your work or studies. They reveal your curiosity and passion. A unique hobby can give you experiences, skills, and stories that you never expected.

Let's break it down with some examples:

Without a Hobby	With a Hobby
Life feels repetitive and routine	Adds excitement and gives you something new to learn
Limited opportunities for personal growth	Teaches new skills and ways to think
Conversations can feel ordinary	Gives you unique stories to share and bond with others

How Hobbies Changed My Life

For me, geopolitics isn't just a subject, it's how I understand the world. My second big hobby, fitness, has taught me how to stay disciplined and work hard. Writing, another hobby, is what led me to create this book.

Hobbies make us human. They give us a break from daily stress and help us see things differently. They're not just activities; they shape who we are. Whether it's painting, fitness, or collecting coins, a hobby can make your life more interesting and meaningful.

If you have a hobby, dive deeper into it. Learn everything you can. And if you don't have one yet, try something new. Who knows? Your hobby might be the key to your next big opportunity.

The Bigger Picture

The best version of yourself is the one who stays true to their dreams, not distracted by others' timelines

CHAPTER 9

BE YOU

Let me clarify something right off the bat: I'm not asking you to be the self-interested person in the world, constantly obsessing over yourself. But there are times when you need to take a step back and think about yourself, your life, your choices, and your dreams.

Why?

Because it's easy to get caught up in what everyone else is doing.

Your friends are enjoying their lives, posting fun short videos on social media.

Someone just went on a vacation to an exotic destination.

One friend bought a premium smartphone, another got a bike, and yet another is happily in a relationship.

It's tempting to compare your life to theirs, but here's the truth: comparison is the thief of joy. Before you get swept away by these distractions, take a moment to pause and reflect.

Who Are You?

Ask yourself some fundamental questions:

What's my current situation?

What's my family's financial status?

What do I truly want to achieve?

If you can answer these questions honestly, you'll gain clarity about what truly matters to you and what doesn't.

This world is full of distractions, from social media trends to peer pressure. But if you can resist these distractions and stay focused on your goals, the universe will align in your favor. The things you dream about will come to you not because of luck, but because of your hard work and persistence.

Let me give you an example. Right now, as you're reading this book, you might think, Oh, this guy just wrote a book; it must have been easy for him. But let me tell you something: I fought with time to deliver this book.

I have a packed schedule, juggling my job, workouts, and personal commitments. But I still made the effort to write every single chapter because I wanted to share my journey with you.

Why? Because I know who I am. I know what I want. And I'm willing to hustle for it, no matter how tough it gets.

Be Yourself

If you want to achieve something whether it's a dream job, financial freedom, or personal growth you need to be yourself first.

Forget about what others are doing. Their life is theirs, and yours is yours. Focus on your journey. Set your goals. Work on them daily. Hustle. And trust me, if you stay true to yourself, you can achieve anything you set your mind to.

The Story of Michael Phelps:

Michael Phelps, the most decorated Olympian of all time, wasn't born a swimming legend. In fact, as a child, he struggled with ADHD and found it hard to focus in school. While many doubted his ability to channel his energy, Phelps discovered a sanctuary in the pool. With the guidance of his coach, Bob Bowman, he built a routine that not only suited his physical strengths but also honed his mental discipline.

What set Phelps apart was his unwavering focus on his journey. While other swimmers might have been distracted by comparisons or rivalries, Phelps trained with a singular mindset: to be the best version of himself. He didn't care about the training schedules or personal bests of his competitors. Instead, he and Bowman developed a unique system—training twice a day, swimming an average of 50 miles a week, and visualizing every possible scenario, including potential failures.

This rigorous preparation was put to the ultimate test during the 2008 Beijing Olympics in the 200m butterfly event. Phelps dove into the water with millions of eyes on him, but midway through the race, his goggles began to fill with water. By the final lap, he was swimming completely blind.

For most swimmers, this would have been a disaster—a moment of panic that could have cost them the race. But not for Phelps. He had prepared for this exact scenario during training. He didn't rely on what he could see; instead, he relied on what he knew. Through relentless practice, Phelps had memorized the exact number of strokes it took to complete each lap. Staying calm, he counted his strokes, trusted his training, and powered through to the finish.

When he touched the wall, he had not only won the gold medal but also set a new world record all while swimming blind.

Phelps didn't succeed because of luck or external validation. He succeeded because he knew himself. He focused on his own goals, trusted his unique preparation, and blocked out the noise of the world around him. This moment is a testament to the power of being true to oneself, staying focused, and never letting external distractions derail your journey.

Just like Phelps, you don't need to see everything clearly to succeed. You just need to trust yourself and your preparation.

In the early stages of your career, chase learning, not earning. Build yourself, and wealth will follow you.

CHAPTER 10

DON'T CHASE

When you're starting out in your career, it's natural to dream about the big paycheck. You see people flashing their cars, exotic vacations, and designer clothes on social media, and it's tempting to think: That's what success looks like. But here's the harsh truth: chasing money early in your career is like chasing a mirage. The harder you run, the further it slips away.

In reality, the early stages of your career aren't about getting rich; they're about building a foundation. This is the time to invest in yourself: learning skills, gaining experience, and making connections that will set you apart in the long run. Money might not flow in abundance right now, but what you're earning is far more valuable for your future potential.

Think about it this way: Would you rather earn a small sum immediately, or spend a few years building yourself into someone who can command far greater rewards for decades to come? The choice is clear. Focus on growth over greed.

Chasing money can also trap you in jobs or situations that don't align with your goals. A higher paycheck might lure you into work that feels meaningless or burns you out. Over time, you'll realize that what truly matters isn't the salary, but the satisfaction and purpose you derive from your work.

The key is to be patient. Hone your craft, create value, and money will eventually find its way to you often in ways you never imagined. As the saying goes, don't chase money; attract it. And the only way to attract it is by becoming the kind of person who's worth investing in.

Let me explain this with my own story.

My Dilemma

I had three offer letters in my hand:

1. An MNC (Multi-National Corporation): High brand value, prestigious name.
2. A Well-Established Company: Steady pay, clear job responsibilities, and stability.
3. A Startup: A small team, uncertain future, lower pay but immense potential for growth.

Choosing the MNC or the well-established company might have made sense to many. With either of those, I would've enjoyed high pay and a comfortable position. But here's the catch:

Limited exposure would have been confined to a single role or department.

Restricted growth, my knowledge and skills would have been siloed.

So, I made what some people might call a "risky" decision: I chose the startup.

Why I Chose the Startup

Broad Exposure: In a startup, you don't just stick to one role; you wear multiple hats. You might work on product development in the morning, marketing in the afternoon, and customer engagement in the evening.

Learning Opportunities: I wanted to learn how businesses are built from the ground up. I wanted to see how departments like sales, marketing, operations, and tech come together to create something valuable.

Creative Freedom: Startups encourage you to think, experiment, and implement. Your ideas aren't lost in a sea of bureaucracy they're heard and acted upon.

Being a Builder: I didn't want to just work for a brand; I wanted to help build one.

The Backlash

When I made my decision, some people questioned me.

"Why would you reject the MNC?"

"Startups are risky; what if it doesn't work out?"

"You're losing a chance for stability and a big paycheck!"

Their concerns were valid, but here's what they didn't see:

I wasn't chasing money or comfort. I was chasing knowledge, experience, and growth. I knew what I wanted for my future, and I wasn't going to settle for a limited path.

Where It Led Me

From being a guy in a tier-3 city to becoming an important team member in a growing startup, my journey has been nothing short of transformative. I've learned more in a few months at the startup than I might have in years at a bigger corporation.

And guess what? The money followed. When you build your skills, knowledge, and network, financial rewards naturally come as a byproduct.

The Moral of the Story

Don't chase money when you're just starting. Chase learning and opportunities instead.

Choose places where you can experiment with your ideas and grow as a professional.

Be willing to work hard and step outside your comfort zone.

The world might tell you to follow the money,
but I'm telling you to follow the path of growth.
If you keep updating yourself, the money will come automatically.

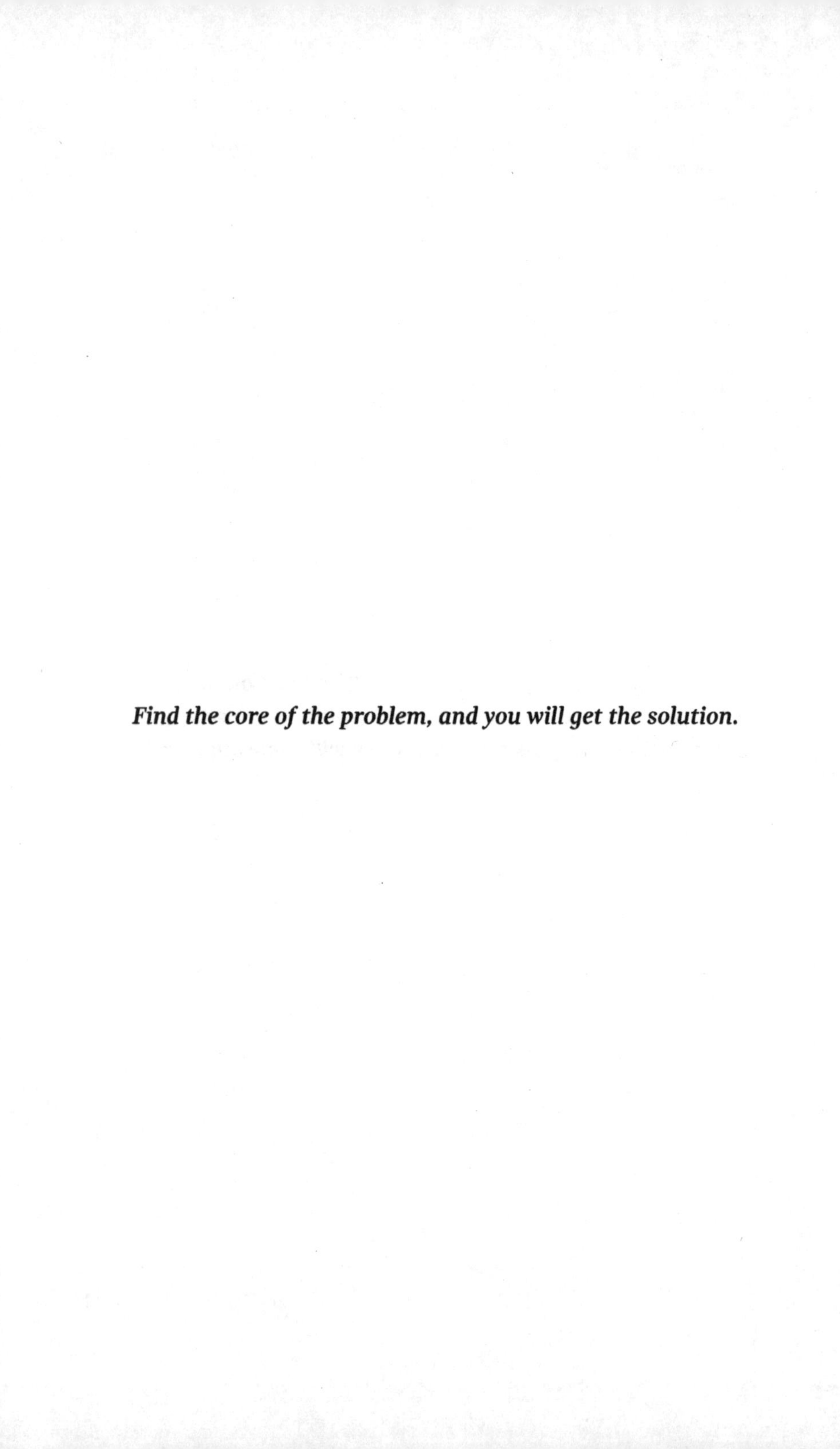

Find the core of the problem, and you will get the solution.

CHAPTER 11

Problem Solving

You can't write the answer during an exam without knowing the question. Similarly, you can't find a solution without understanding the core of the problem.

Once, I had the opportunity to deliver a guest lecture on problem-solving in front of more than 130 students. I accepted the opportunity without much thought. But there was a catch. I was someone who hesitated to communicate even with the bus conductor to get my balance back. The irony? Now I was expected to talk confidently to a crowd.

During the lecture, I shared my personal struggle with communication and how it became a "problem" in various situations. When I asked the students about the core of my issue, they unanimously said, "Lack of communication." I smiled and pointed out, "Then what am I doing right now?" They all laughed and replied, "Solving it!"

That's when I introduced them to my Problem-Solving Loop:

Jump in → Find → Try → Fail → Learn → Retry → Solve.

1. Jump In

The first step is to stop avoiding the problem and face it directly. No matter how intimidating or complex the issue might appear, acknowledging it is crucial. Taking that initial leap of courage to engage with the problem is where the journey begins. Many people stay stuck because they never take this step, but solutions are only possible when you begin.

2. Find

Once you're in, you need to identify the root cause. This isn't always as straightforward as it seems; surface-level symptoms often hide deeper issues. By digging deeper, observing, analyzing, and reflecting you can uncover what truly needs to be addressed. Without understanding the core, any solution will be superficial.

3. Try

Armed with clarity about the issue, it's time to act. This is your chance to experiment and test potential solutions. It doesn't matter if your approach isn't perfect at first, what matters is moving forward and making an attempt.

4. Fail

Failure is an inevitable part of problem-solving. It's not a sign of defeat but a necessary checkpoint. Failure provides critical feedback, showing you what doesn't work and highlighting areas for improvement. Instead of fearing it, embrace it as a stepping stone toward progress.

5. Learn

Every failure carries a lesson. By analyzing what went wrong, you gain insights that refine your understanding of the problem and improve your approach. This phase is where growth happens; each setback is an opportunity to learn and prepare better for the next step.

6. Retry

With new insights in hand, you try again. But this time, it's not just about repeating the process, it's about iterating with a smarter, more informed approach. Persistence and adaptation are the key ingredients here, helping you get closer to the solution with each attempt.

7. Solve

After navigating through the loop—trying, failing, learning, and retrying—you reach a point where the problem is either solved or significantly mitigated. The solution may not be perfect, but it's the result of deliberate effort, persistence, and a willingness to adapt.

Why This Loop Works

The problem-solving loop isn't just a framework; it's a mindset. It teaches you to embrace failure, value effort, and focus on growth. By following this approach, you'll find that even the most daunting challenges can be broken down and tackled systematically.

This loop taught me that nothing is impossible to overcome if we break the problem down to its root. By identifying the core issue, we can experiment, fail, and eventually solve it.

So, what's the core of your problem today?
Think about it, your solution might just be one loop away.

Money isn't just numbers; it's a reflection of your decisions. Start early, diversify smartly, and let compounding quietly build your wealth over time.

CHAPTER 12

The Finance

When it comes to personal finance, the sooner you start, the better. Why? Because of the magic of compounding and the long-term benefits of disciplined investing. Here's my story:

At 19, I decided to jump into the stock market. On June 9, 2023, I opened my Demat account. I had no idea how brokerage apps worked or what terms like "intraday," "delivery," or "SIP" meant. But instead of overthinking, I started small, really small. With ₹100, I purchased penny stocks in two different modes just to see how things worked.

This small step cost me ₹100 in testing, but it gave me priceless knowledge. I learned how to buy, hold, and sell stocks and understood the workflows of a brokerage app. Once I got the basics down, I started saving stocks in my watchlist after thorough research.

A week later, I attended a free workshop on stock market investments. It opened my eyes to terms like SIP (Systematic Investment Plan), gold bonds, S&P 500, and more. Armed with this newfound knowledge, I took my investments seriously.

Building My Portfolio

Within a year, I grew my portfolio to a five-digit investment with a four-digit return. But I quickly realized buying individual stocks with small holdings wasn't giving me consistent returns. That's when I turned to SIPs.

I selected five different mutual funds and began investing ₹100 in each every month. These five funds were diversified across categories to minimize risk. For five months, I monitored their performance. The market was volatile due to elections and geopolitical tensions, but I learned to stay calm and focus on the long-term picture.

After the testing phase, I discontinued two funds that consistently underperformed and doubled down on the remaining three. This taught me an important lesson: diversification isn't just about reducing risk; it's about optimizing opportunities.

Why Diversification is Key

Diversification applies not only to investments but to life as a whole. Just as a diversified portfolio balances risk and return, having a varied skill set prepares you for unexpected challenges and new opportunities. If you can master personal finance and diversification early, you'll have the tools to solve half of life's problems.

What You Should Learn

Start Early: Even if you invest ₹100, the habit and experience will pay off in the long run.

Understand Compounding: Small, consistent investments grow exponentially over time.

Learn About SIPs: Systematic Investment Plans are a great way to build wealth steadily.

Distinguish Assets from Liabilities: Real assets appreciate and generate income, while liabilities drain your wealth.

Diversify: Spread your investments across different asset classes and categories.

My Method: Practical Learning

I'm a hands-on learner. Instead of waiting for the "perfect time," I took risks and learned from them. That's how I built my financial discipline. My ₹100 experiment grew into a confident understanding of personal finance.

You can do the same. Start small, stay patient, and keep learning. It's not just about building wealth; it's about building a foundation for a peaceful and financially secure life.

Finance isn't complicated, it's a habit. Whether it's investing, budgeting, or planning, the earlier you start, the better your future will look. So, jump in, learn from your mistakes, and watch your financial knowledge and portfolio grow.

Why I Stopped Buying Stocks and the Issue with Single-Digit Holdings

In the initial stages of my investment journey, I was fascinated by the stock market and bought individual shares of different companies. Like most beginners, I believed that spreading my money across multiple companies would reduce risk. However, as I gained experience, I realized that this strategy wasn't as effective as I had imagined. Here's why:

1. **Lack of Impact with Single-Digit Holdings**
   When you buy just one or two shares of multiple companies, the returns you earn barely make a difference to your overall portfolio. For example:
   If a share priced at ₹100 grows by 10%, your ₹100 investment earns ₹10.
   Even if it grows by 50%, your profit is ₹50.
   While the percentage may look exciting, the absolute return is negligible unless you own a significant quantity of shares.
2. **Fragmented Portfolio**
   Owning single-digit shares in multiple companies results in a scattered portfolio that's hard to manage. Instead of focusing on a few quality investments, I was spreading myself too thin, making it difficult to track performance, understand company fundamentals, and make informed decisions.
3. **No Meaningful Growth**
   Growth in the stock market is driven by the power of compounding, which requires consistent reinvestment and focus. Spreading a small amount of capital across too many companies prevents any single investment from growing meaningfully.

4. **High Transaction Costs**
   When you buy and sell shares frequently or in small quantities, transaction fees and brokerage charges eat into your returns. The smaller the investment, the larger the impact of these costs.

Why I Shifted My Strategy

After understanding these challenges, I decided to adopt a more focused and disciplined approach. Here's what I did instead:

1. **Started SIPs in Mutual Funds**
   Instead of buying individual stocks, I began investing in mutual funds through Systematic Investment Plans (SIPs). Here's why:
   Mutual funds pool money from multiple investors to invest in a diversified portfolio of stocks, bonds, or other assets.
   Professional fund managers make informed decisions, reducing the risk for individual investors like me.
   SIPs allow me to invest consistently, benefiting from rupee cost averaging and compounding returns over time.
2. **Focused on Quality Over Quantity**
   I decided to hold fewer stocks but invest more in each. For example:
   Instead of buying one or two shares of 10 companies, I invested in 3-4 companies with a significant amount.
   This approach helped me build meaningful positions in companies I believed in, maximizing returns from their growth.
3. **Diversification Through Mutual Funds**
   Rather than manually diversifying my portfolio across sectors, I let mutual funds do the work. Each mutual fund is already diversified, spreading risk across multiple companies and industries.
   Equity Funds have exposure to the stock market.
   Debt Funds balanced my portfolio with safer investments.

Index Funds mirrored the performance of indices like Nifty 50 or Sensex.

4. **Better Monitoring and Time Management**

   Managing a smaller number of quality investments allowed me to spend more time understanding them. For the rest of my portfolio, I trusted mutual funds to handle diversification and growth.

   Buying single-digit shares of multiple companies might seem like a good strategy at first, but it's not effective in the long run. The stock market rewards focus, patience, and consistency. By shifting to mutual funds and concentrating on quality investments, I not only simplified my portfolio but also maximized its potential for growth.

   This isn't to say you should avoid stocks entirely, just make sure your approach is deliberate, well-researched, and focused on long-term wealth creation.

Compounding: The Wealth Multiplier

Imagine this: You plant a single mango seed today. You water it, take care of it, and wait patiently. Over time, the seed grows into a tree, and one day, it starts giving you hundreds of mangoes year after year. What if I told you that money could do the same thing? That's the power of compounding your money earned, and then those earnings earn even more, creating a snowball effect of growth.

How Does Compounding Work?

Let's bring in Ramesh Uncle, your middle-class neighbor who loved his evening tea and pakoras. One day, someone told him, "If you save ₹1,000 a month for 20 years and invest it wisely, you could have ₹10 lakhs or more."

Ramesh Uncle thought, "₹1,000 isn't much, it's just my monthly tea shop expense." So, he gave it a try, and by his retirement, he wasn't sitting in a tea shop anymore he owned one.

The Math Behind It:

If you invest ₹1,000 every month at a 12% annual return:

In 10 years, you'd have ₹2.3 lakhs.

In 20 years, it becomes ₹9.3 lakhs.

In 30 years? A jaw-dropping ₹35 lakhs.

What changed? Time and patience. The longer you let your money grow, the harder compounding works.

The Magic of Starting Early

Now, let's introduce Priya and Rahul.

Priya started investing ₹1,000 a month at age 25 and stopped at 35. She invested for 10 years and let the money grow until she turned 60.

Rahul, on the other hand, started at 35 and invested the same ₹1,000/month until he turned 60 (25 years!).

Who has more money at 60? Surprisingly, Priya, even though she invested for a shorter time. That's the magic of starting early. Your money gets more time to compound.

What Investments Offer Compounding Returns?

Compounding isn't limited to just the stock market. Here's where you can see it in action:

1. **SIPs (Systematic Investment Plans):** Regular investments in mutual funds.
2. **Fixed Deposits (FDs):** Though returns are lower, compounding works over time.
3. **Public Provident Fund (PPF):** A government-backed scheme that grows your money tax-free.
4. **Dividend Stocks:** Reinvesting dividends can turbocharge your returns.

Why Are We Afraid of Compounding?

People often say, "What's the point of saving ₹500? It's so small." But here's the truth: small habits lead to big outcomes. Would you skip watering that mango tree just because it doesn't give fruit immediately? Then why skip investing small amounts?

Compounding is your silent, hardworking employee. The earlier you hire it, the richer you'll be.

SIP & SWP: The Dynamic Duo of Financial Growth

Let's talk about SIP (Systematic Investment Plan) and SWP (Systematic Withdrawal Plan). If compounding is the engine of wealth creation, SIP and SWP are the drivers who make sure you stay on track.

What Is SIP?

SIP is like planting seeds every month instead of all at once. It allows you to invest small amounts regularly in mutual funds or other assets, making it easier to grow wealth without burning a hole in your pocket.

How Does SIP Work?

Picture this: Manoj, a 25-year-old software engineer, decides to invest ₹5,000 every month in an equity mutual fund via SIP. The market has its ups and downs, but Manoj doesn't stop. Over 20 years, his ₹12 lakhs investment (₹5,000 x 12 months x 20 years) turns into ₹50 lakhs at a 12% annual return.

Why? SIP allows you to buy more units when the market is low and fewer units when it's high, averaging your investment cost (rupee cost averaging).

Why Is Long-Term SIP Important?

The longer you stay, the better compounding works. Think of SIP as a marathon, not a sprint. It gives you:

1. **Discipline:** You invest regularly without worrying about timing the market.
2. **Wealth Creation:** Even small amounts grow into a significant corpus over time.
3. **Peace of Mind:** You let the market's volatility work in your favor instead of stressing over it.

SIP for Early Retirement

Imagine retiring at 45 instead of 60. Sounds dreamy, right? SIP makes this possible. For example, investing ₹10,000 per month from age 25 to 45 at a 12% annual return can give you over ₹1.5 crore. That's enough to design a life of freedom and pursue your passions without financial stress.

What Is SWP?

While SIP helps you grow wealth, SWP ensures you enjoy it. Think of SWP as your financial retirement paycheck; it allows you to withdraw a fixed amount regularly from your investments, ensuring a steady income.

How Does SWP Work?

Take Rita Aunty, who retired with ₹50 lakhs in her mutual fund portfolio. Instead of withdrawing it all at once, she sets up an SWP to withdraw ₹30,000 per month. The remaining amount stays invested and keeps growing.

Benefits of SWP:

1. **Steady Income:** Perfect for retirement or any phase where you need regular money.
2. **Tax Efficiency:** Only the capital gains portion is taxed, unlike a fixed deposit where the entire amount is taxable.
3. **Wealth Preservation:** Your principal amount continues to grow, ensuring you don't run out of money.

The SIP-SWP Connection

Here's the real beauty: What you build with SIP, you enjoy with SWP. SIP plants the tree, and SWP lets you enjoy its fruits without cutting it down.

Let's Do the Math

Start a SIP of ₹5,000/month for 20 years at 12% return = ₹50 lakhs.

Set up an SWP of ₹25,000/month for 20 years post-retirement = ₹60 lakhs withdrawn while still preserving your principal.

SIP and SWP are tools to design a life where your money works harder than you do. They're not just financial strategies, they're lifestyle enablers. Start small, stay consistent, and let them shape your financial freedom.

Real Asset vs. Liability: Know the Difference to Grow Your Wealth

If SIP and SWP are your financial superheroes, understanding real assets and liabilities is like figuring out their backstory. It's crucial to know the difference because what you think is an asset could actually be a liability eating away at your wealth.

What Is a Real Asset?

A real asset is something that puts money into your pocket over time. It appreciates in value or generates income. Think of it as a golden goose that keeps laying eggs without asking for much in return.

Examples of Real Assets:

1. **Stocks & Mutual Funds:** Grow over time and offer returns.
2. **Real Estate (Rental Property):** Generates rent and appreciates in value.
3. **Gold:** A hedge against inflation, though it doesn't generate regular income.
4. **Businesses:** If managed well, they produce consistent cash flow.
5. **Your Skills:** Yes, upskilling is an asset. It enhances your earning potential.

What Is Liability?

A liability is something that takes money out of your pocket. It might look shiny and desirable, but it's a financial drain in disguise.

Examples of Liabilities:

1. **Cars:** Depreciate the moment you buy them and come with fuel and maintenance costs.
2. **Gadgets:** The latest phone may look cool, but it won't pay your bills.
3. **Loans for Non-Essential Items:** Credit card debt for vacations or luxury items.
4. **Overpriced Real Estate:** A fancy house that doesn't generate income but burns money through EMIs, maintenance, and taxes.

A Real-Life Story: Arjun vs. Raghav

Let me introduce you to two friends: Arjun and Raghav.

Arjun buys a ₹12 lakh car at 25, taking a loan for it. He spends ₹20,000 per month on EMIs and ₹10,000 on fuel and maintenance. By 30, the car is worth ₹3 lakh, and he's out of ₹15 lakh (including expenses).

Raghav invests the same ₹12 lakh in a small rental property. It gives him ₹15,000/month in rent, which grows to ₹25,000/month by the time he's 30. The property value also appreciates to ₹20 lakh.

Who's better off? Raghav, because he chose a real asset that grows instead of a liability that depreciates.

How to Identify Real Assets and Liabilities in Your Life

Ask yourself these questions:

1. Does it appreciate over time? If yes, it's likely an asset.
2. Does it generate income? If yes, it's a real asset.
3. Does it lose value and require continuous spending? If yes, it's a liability.

Common Myths About Assets and Liabilities

1. **"My house is my biggest asset."**
   Not unless it's generating rent. Your primary residence is often a liability because of maintenance costs, property tax, and EMIs.
2. **"Luxury items show my status."**

Status is temporary; debt is long-lasting. That designer watch won't pay your bills.

3. **"Gold is outdated."**
   Gold may not generate regular income, but it's a reliable store of value in tough times.

Flip Your Liabilities

Look around your life and list your liabilities.

Can you turn any of them into assets?

For example:

Turn your spare room into an Airbnb rental.

Upskill to increase your earning potential.

Sell old items you don't use and invest the money.

The Takeaway: Build a Life of Assets

If you want financial freedom, focus on acquiring income-generating assets and minimizing liabilities. The earlier you understand this, the faster you'll grow your wealth.

Real assets are like bricks for your financial foundation, while liabilities are cracks in the wall. Build wisely, and your financial house will stand strong for years to come.

Personal Finance Formula: The Blueprint for Financial Freedom

When it comes to managing money, most people either wing it or follow outdated advice. But personal finance isn't rocket science, it's about understanding and applying a simple formula consistently. Let's break it down step by step, keeping it practical, relatable, and, of course, engaging.

The Formula

Earnings – Spending = Savings

Savings + Investments = Wealth

The goal? To ensure your wealth grows steadily over time while keeping liabilities in check. Sounds easy, right? Let's dive deeper.

Step 1: Master Your Earnings

You can't save or invest what you don't earn. Your income is the fuel for your financial engine.

Active Income: Your salary, freelance gigs, or any work that requires your time.

Passive Income: Income from rental properties, dividends, SIP returns, or side hustles.

Tip: Always look for ways to diversify your income streams. If your salary is the only source, one layoff could turn your financial life upside down.

Step 2: Control Your Spending

Earnings are limited, but desires? Unlimited. That's why you need to differentiate between needs and wants.

Needs: Rent, groceries, healthcare.

Wants: The latest iPhone, a vacation in the Maldives.

Golden Rule: Follow the 50-30-20 rule.

50% for needs.

30% for wants.

20% for savings and investments.

If your "wants" dominate your spending, you're setting yourself up for financial stress.

Step 3: Build and Boost Savings

Savings are your financial safety net. It's what stands between you and debt during emergencies.

Start with an emergency fund: 3–6 months' worth of expenses.

Automate your savings: Treat it like a monthly bill you owe yourself.

Why Save? Because without savings, you'll never have the funds to invest. And without investing, compounding can't work its magic.

Step 4: Invest Smartly

Savings are great, but investments grow your wealth. This is where all those SIPs, SWPs, and compounding topics come into play.

Short-Term Goals: Use low-risk options like fixed deposits or liquid mutual funds.

Long-Term Goals: SIP in equity funds, real estate, or even gold.

Remember: Inflation is a silent killer. Your money sitting in a savings account loses value every day. Invest it to outpace inflation and build wealth.

Step 5: Understand Assets vs. Liabilities

We just covered this, but here's the recap:

Real Assets: Stocks, mutual funds, rental properties, skills.

Liabilities: Anything that drains money (fancy cars, impulsive loans).

The formula for wealth: More assets, fewer liabilities.

Step 6: Monitor and Optimize

Managing personal finance is not a one-time task. You need to monitor your progress and adjust based on your goals.

Track Your Expenses: Apps like Walnut or Excel sheets can help.

Review Your Portfolio: Check your investments quarterly.

Upgrade Your Knowledge: Read books, attend workshops, or follow market trends.

A Relatable Story: The Tale of Meera and Her Formula

Meera, a school teacher, used to live paycheck to paycheck. One day, her 12-year-old son asked her why she always said, "We can't afford that." Embarrassed and motivated, Meera decided to turn her financial life around.

She followed the personal finance formula:

Cut down her expenses by 20% by canceling unused subscriptions and cooking at home.

Started a ₹1,000 SIP monthly and created an emergency fund.

Picked up freelance tutoring on weekends, adding ₹10,000 to her income.

Learned about the stock market and shifted her savings into high-performing mutual funds.

In just 5 years, Meera saved ₹8 lakhs, paid off her debts, and started planning an early retirement.

Create Your Formula

Take a moment to reflect:

1. What's your earning potential?
2. Where can you cut unnecessary spending?
3. Are you saving enough to start investing?

Create your personalized financial formula today. Start small, stay consistent, and watch your wealth grow.

The Takeaway

The personal finance formula isn't about making millions overnight. It's about discipline, patience, and smart decisions. If you master this formula early, financial freedom is within your reach.

Ask yourself:

Are you controlling your money, or is it controlling you?
What steps can you take today to secure a wealthier tomorrow?

Your financial success starts with the formula, but it thrives on your actions. Let's make them count!

Conclusion

WHY NOT?

And here we are, the final chapter of this book. Before you close it and move on, let me ask you one question: Why not?

Why not dream big? Why not take that first step? Why not keep going even when everything feels like it's falling apart?

Let me tell you something if someone like me, who couldn't pass all his school exams, could:

Write multiple articles that people actually read.

Become a core team member of a startup.

Deliver guest lectures in front of students .

Publish this book that you're reading now.

Then why not you?

Recap of the Journey

This book isn't just a collection of chapters; it's a basic blueprint, a reflection of the struggles, lessons, and breakthroughs that shape success. Let's revisit what we've covered:

Why I Write This Book

I shared my purpose for writing this book. It's not about me, it's about you, and the journey we're about to take together.

Am I Even Qualified to Write This Book?

I addressed the elephant in the room: what makes me think I can write a book? The answer? Experience and lessons learned the hard way.

The Essential Powers for Growth

Chapter 1: Power of Cravings

Understanding your desires can either drive you or distract you.

Chapter 2: Power of Fear

Fear isn't your enemy; it's your guide. Learn to use it, not run from it.

Chapter 3: Power of Patience

In a world of instant gratification, patience is your biggest asset.

Chapter 4: Power of Personal Branding

Your reputation precedes you. Build it intentionally, one step at a time.

Life's Core Principles

Chapter 5: Consistency Over Motivation

Forget fleeting motivation. Consistency is what gets results.

Chapter 6: Why Geopolitics

The world isn't just about you. Understanding it broadens your perspective.

Chapter 7: Why Risk

No risk, no reward. Calculated risks are the stepping stones to growth.

Chapter 8: Why Hobbies

Your hobbies aren't just a pastime, they're an escape and a creative boost.

The Bigger Picture

Chapter 9: Be You

Stop trying to fit into boxes. Be unapologetically yourself.

Chapter 10: Don't Chase

What's meant for you will come if you focus on growth instead of chasing.

Chapter 11: Problem-Solving

Life throws problems, but you've got the tools to tackle them head-on.

Chapter 12: Finance

Master your money. Start early, be disciplined, and watch your wealth grow.

Why Not You?

It's easy to say, "I can't do it," but let me remind you of one thing: Everyone starts somewhere. Nobody is born an expert. If I, with all my setbacks and struggles, could push through, you can too.

Life will throw challenges at you. People will doubt you. You'll doubt yourself. But every small effort adds up. Every failure is just a step closer to success.

When others see your success, they might say it happened overnight. But you'll know the truth. You'll know the sleepless nights, the sacrifices, and the persistence that got you there.

What's Next?

This book isn't an end, it's the beginning of your journey. Take the lessons you've learned from these chapters and apply them. Start small, but start today.

Why not take the first step toward your goals?
Why not believe in yourself?
Why not keep going, even when it's tough?
Signing Off

Let me leave you with this:

It might seem like you're stuck.
It might feel like nothing is working.
But keep pushing, keep going, and keep hustling.
You'll look back one day and thank yourself for not giving up.
This is your journey, and you're the one in control. If I can do it, why not you?

Let's go. The world is waiting for you :)

www.ingramcontent.com/pod-product-compliance
Lightning Source LLC
LaVergne TN
LVHW041116150826
845673LV00007B/2077

* 9 7 9 8 8 9 7 2 4 6 5 4 0 *